Caffeinated

by Annette Gagliardi

September 26, 2024

Island of Wak-Wak

Island of Wak-Wak
Örebro, Sweden
www.islandofwakwak.com

October 2024

Cover Photograph: by Annette Gagliardi.
Model: Maggie Gagliardi
Cover Clip Art: by SVG Repo
www.svgrepo.com

Typeset using KOMA-Script & LaTeX 2_ε.
Printed via Books on Demand.
www.bod.se

ISBN: 978-9198959826

Contents

Acknowledgments

"Comfort" was first published in "Poems Around Us," *Gideon Poetry Review* on April 2020.

"Cookin'" was first published in the May 2023 issue of *Down in the Dirt* magazine (Volume 207, released 5/1/23).

"Gourmand of Orange" was first published in the *Pasque Petals*, spring 2020, South Dakota State Poetry Society.

"I Thought I Loved Your Breakfast Bacon" was first published April/May 2019 in *Foliate Oak Literary Magazine.*

"More Please" (previously untitled) was first published by *Door Is A Jar Magazine* in Issue 13, Winter 2020.

"One Balmy Evening" was first published in the *Southwest Journal*, July 2019.

"'Tis Morning" was first published in *Best Poets of 2018*, Eber & Weir Publishing.

"You Can't Always Sit in the Corner Booth" was first published in *Meat for Tea: The Valley Review*, Volume 17, Issue 2, June 2023.

"You Lucky Dog" was first published in the *Southwest Journal*, 2015.

All photographs of coffee signage come from a collection owned by Hannah Ezell, Anchorage, Alaska. Used with permission.

Preface

This collection pays homage to the beverages we so love to wake up to, so love to enjoy throughout the day, in many ways, and that we so love to imbibe before bed. Sunny and funny poems are interspersed with more serious ones that provide a punch, because coffee helps us think deep thoughts. Yet we don't want to take ourselves too seriously. The book ends the collection with a couple poems full of gratitude for the day and the availability of caffeine, in its many forms.

Prologue

Historians suggest that caffeine was consumed as far back as 2737 BC when Chinese Emperor Shen Nung boiled drinking water and leaves from a nearby bush, creating a pleasant aroma and the first pot of tea.[1]

The word, *caffeine* was derived from the German word *kaffee* and the French word *café*, each meaning coffee. According to the FDA, "caffeine can be part of a healthy diet for most people."

The American Institute for Cancer Research recommends drinking coffee "regularly" and concludes that coffee lowers risk of liver and endometrial cancers.

The Journal of the American Medical Association (JAMA) says caffeine can increase alertness, decrease fatigue, and improve reaction times. It may also help reduce appetite, and prevent weight gain.

In a large study looking at over 400,000 people, coffee consumption was associated with lower likelihood of death from disease.[2]

JAMA has concluded that consumption of both caffeinated and decaffeinated coffee is associated with decreased risk of death overall, as well as with reduced risk of type 2 diabetes, Parkinson's disease, liver disease and multiple types of cancer.[3]

People have been drinking tea for 5,000 years. It is the second most-consumed beverage in the world (water is number one).

Research shows that drinking black tea reduces the risk of stroke, improves focus, lowers blood-sugar levels, promotes heart health, and decreases the risk of some cancers. In short, drinking tea lessens the risk of death from all causes.

[1] Arab and Blumberg 2008.

[2] "Association of Coffee Drinking with Total and Cause-Specific Mortality" by Freedman, Park, Abnet, Hollenbeck and Sinha in *The New England Journal of Medicine* (2012) (taken from: `https://www.nejm.org/doi/full/10.1056/NEJMoa1112010`).

[3] from: `https://www.ncausa.org/About-Coffee/Coffee-Health`.

Caffeinated

Coffea

Coffee — the favorite drink of the civilized world.

Thomas Jefferson

Discovered by an Ethiopian goatherd's
galloping goats chewed the beans
filled with caffeine,
and danced — yes, they danced.

The abbot of the monastery
accepted, then cooked the beans
filled with caffeine,
and danced — yes, he danced.

The papal approval came
in 1615, a satisfied populace
gathered, drank their fill
and danced — yes, they danced.

Coffee houses offered patrons
cups and bowls of caffeination's
brewed libation
and danced — yes, they danced.

Small, terraced gardens of family farms —
green waxy leaves, fruit and blossoms
advance in a continuous cycle,
to help us dance — yes, we dance.

I wondered, after being awakened

(*Inspired by* **The Awakening Sculpture** *in Washington, DC.*)

—how does it end?
He's screaming, you know—
a long silent scream   lofted up and out.
Maybe he doesn't want to wake—given
that slumber had been restful—peaceful, even.
What clarion call aroused this being
from the depths of sand and soil?

Is it painful,
this coming up from down under?
Has he been buried alive, struggling just now,
to gain access to the air?
Does he see something sinister
that he needs to escape—thus the clawing?

Open mouth, in mid-shriek gives the impression . . . *all is not well.*

I imagine myself underground in sleep,
trying to gain vantage
from the solid, enclosure of slumber's earth,
trying to pull myself out
of the clutch of such density.

I wonder if I would also be screaming—scratching
toward the lightness and breeze of air, pulling parts
of my body from the solid surface;
straining to purchase freedom
from the glued thickness —to separate my specific mass
from the **bulky tightness** of shut-eye.

Would I feel the necessity of rousing
to the next level, OUT of the weight
of this slumber's atmosphere?

Is there a deep need to crawl/ scrape/ clutch
from this firmament, into the heavens—the universe—the cosmos?

Or,   is he just **rising** in urgent need of his first cup of Joe?—Calling out
to anyone who might have some fresh brew to share.

Cookin'

Clouds passing overhead are hot-muffin
mountains scorching the sky.

Each small puff of thought a disintegrating
cinnamon toast in warm milk.

It melts in your mouth,
slides over your tongue

and slithers down your throat
to collapsed in jellied ear canals.

Eyes that sniff sassafras and fern leaf tea are black
holes that gobble and expel a closet full of cats

chasing a belled figment. Each filament, a tangled,
elusive myth on the threshold of truth.

Dreams sandwiched between night
terrors stuffed into emotional eclairs

clog and clutter until there
is nowhere to flee save the deflated

cake-like comfort of bed, glossed
with the iced gash of a morning

full of heady thunder clouds—
a mouthful of morning.

Morning Wakeup

!

I dream my tortoiseshell cat, covered with
a light fuzz of pink grass, pads across my bed,
my body, my head, then slinks between
the brittle morning light and the
smell of freshly roasted coffee.

The coffee is wonderfully predictable.
My softly persistent cat marks the carpet
with tufts of fur and finds
her spot in my chair. I look
out the window at the dry brown land.
I drink from this hot, bitter place.

I cannot meet the morning without
my hot Mocha. The caffeine reaching
my veins, rousing me from slumber,
clears my mind of any leftover
dreams and reminds me of who I am.

%

The day materializes in my
consciousness as I empty my cup.
Any mention of my cat (*whose
soft fur and mellow purr calms me*) is a mere
fabrication. I am, in fact, allergic.

Dawn's Brew: First Cup

Above the whipped-cream spiral,
my coffee exhales. Dawn slips between
ghosts of early morning mist like a soul

unseen. Shades of purple color the sky.
I yawn and stretch to escape sleep, and sigh
while wondering why I don't linger.

I smell my coffee, dawn's formal "black tie"
— an invitation to live, sans my dreaming.
Today's surge begins its steadfast journey.

The brew in my cup is drunk up, PELL-MELL;
Like a rung bell. The day has arrived,
a fresh start to all I can/must/want to do.

And you, my savory brew, you're swell—
holding my morning together like glue.

Day Break's Second Cup

From the milk spiral lacing
my morning coffee
I see the dawn stroll between
branches of morning mist.

Ever soft and slow slips the stream
of today, on its steadfast journey.
Smell the dew rising — smell
the aroma of dawn.

The brew in my cup
is drunk up — FAST.

It doesn't last
as long as I want it to.
Dawn's stroll doesn't either.

The day has arrived —
an unwelcome intruder
upon the roll of quiet

dawn, which
dissipates
wholly — leaving
my cup empty.

'Tis morning
(***With a nod to Lewis Carroll's "Jabberwocky"***)

and the little chap
does want a bite to eat.
He wants a snorkel bandersnatch;
He wants a bit of meat.

And with his chubby hackensack
he wanders 'round the house
to find a frumpled featherworst;
to stifle him a grouse.

Oh fend thy way, my beamish boy;
Oh fend thy way ashore.
Swim past the oyster bed convoy,
for surely there is more.

Now, rumpus round the evernought
and rumpus round the troy;
then sit thee down and rest a bit,
and then thy food enjoy!

Gourmand of Orange

It was orange:
cold, and round,
and sweet.

He bit into it like someone
eating their last meal,
savoring the lush treat,
licking the dripping rind,
smacking his lips as he
appreciated the tangy aroma.

He sucked the color from the
room as easily as that tangerine—
its ripped rind left
lying on a white napkin—
his attention diverted
from the fruit.

He sucked the orange off
the roses, there on the table,
        arranged so elegantly in the silver teapot
        with an organza ribbon tied 'round.
He sipped the fragrance as he went,
nodding a soft reply to my argument.

Yet, he had no awareness
of how he left things;
how the tangerine was left lacking its color—
the residue dry and smooth as a coffin.

The air was thinned to a wisp,
with others left to gasp
for the remainder;

the flowers devoid of perfume
or hue, washed and wasted—

even the ribbon left defiled and
distant—tarnishing the teapot.

An Ode to Cacao

What flavors in my past lay dead and dry,
    save the taste of cacao bean's bold refrain
    that makes me want to taste again and again—
to savor the flavor, then to sigh
with cocoa's natural, endorphin high.
    What health benefits do I have to gain—
    save the occasional chocolate stain,
one touch upon my tongue, a sweet reply.

That rich, dark chocolate, my destiny
    purchased by the ounce, or by the ton,
this Mayan import's luxury.
The light of day's industrious bee,
    have spent my hours 'til they are done
    and find my chocolate rewards, one by one.

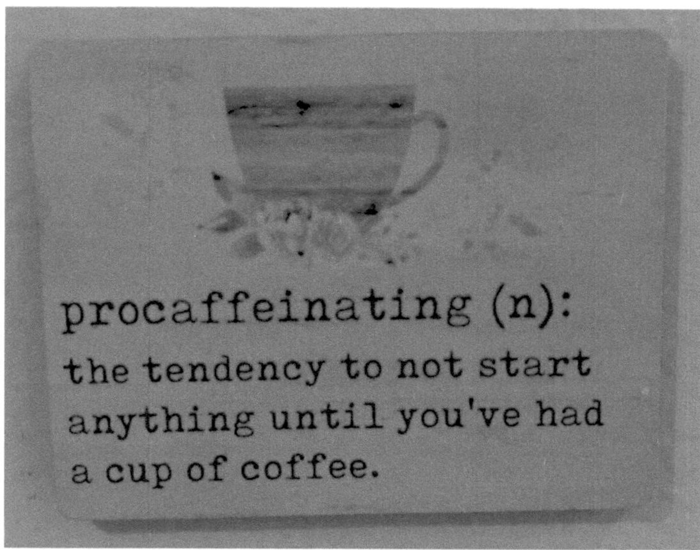

Caffeination

Gnawing the brew,
time after time,
recognizing the clue
that generates the spark & vitality,
narrowly defining our frothy
desire.   Considered
the oldest metabolic pathway—
effervescence bubbles to the top;

livens the slumbering spirit
we wish to incite, to rise
and provoke tastebuds to simmer.

Each enzyme action a
zymology[4] of new brew;
crystalline compounds
with acidic flavors, exotic
compounds metabolic
enhancement—stimulates!

Energy released!

[4] *zymology* (the science of fermentation)

I Thought I Loved Your Breakfast Bacon

It isn't the sound
of the sizzle
as edges brown,

the tantalizing aroma
that blends
with my mocha,

nor the first crisp bite
making my mouth
water and savor salted delight.

now I realize it isn't the bacon
taste I love, nor the
time or care taken,

but the linger
of salt on your lips,
your skin, my fingers

after we've eaten.

You Lucky Dog

Another morning,
I struggle to feel alive.

The dog snoring softly on our bedroom rug,
    content and peaceful in his repose
    doesn't rise,
    as I do, stumbling in the dark
    to eliminate the nights' accumulation.

His dream continues into the warming of the day
    with mementos of past victories
    while I drag myself awake,
    move soundlessly through rooms,
    dig in closets, and eat alone.

Some vague fantasy plays itself out in his mind, as
    I gather work paraphernalia and food
    for a second meal of the day
    and make my way
    to the door.

Good-bye — and sweet dreams,
    you lucky dog.

Tip the Cup

What magic, this taste
of the best brew
in the place?

This seed of sublime
sensory pick-up is no ordinary
cherry bean. It creates

a beverage to activate,
motivate, and promises longer life
with less strife, in the process.

A strong cup of espresso that slaps you
in the face, makes your eyes open
wide and kicks you out of bed,

while making you smile
with satisfaction as the aroma
and flavors fulfill your needs.

Our Daily Excess

"*We've lost whole octaves of feeling.*"[5]
All the quiet emotions are less than whispers.

Oh, yes. Fear, outrage, excitement are loud and proud.
You can hear them around town,

See them spill all over social media,
the newspapers and television talk shows.

You just don't know if all that *high*
ripe is really real.

Yet, the quiet delight, the contented lament
of a soft-spoken recognition is barely audible anymore.

We are trapped in the amphitheater
of extravagant emotional indulgence.

Instead of speaking our truth in quiet assurance,
we shout it loud and long in a variety of spaces and places.

The excessive exaggeration
of offenses past and present

leap off the page and out of digital
devices delivering the daily extra.

What ever happened to moderation?

[5] Sr. Mara Faulkner, O.S.B. at LOMP conference in St. Cloud, MN on April 28, 2018

I Saw You

I saw you standing there;
waiting in the coffee line,
drenched —
water dripping . . .

I should have
stopped,
but didn't.
Forgive me . . .

I too, was
waiting in the coffee line,
drenched —
water dripping . . .

(*I was*) so, so cold —
impatiently waiting —
caffeine headache throbbing
— water dripping.

Worker Bees

Like lemmings to the sea,
to early coffee houses,
with work masks in place,
and steady workers' pace—
they wait for their jolt awake.

A thousand tramping feet
press out into the street
ten thousand hands and heads
blend mind and soul and beat—
then transport from home to work.

Ten thousand eyes & ears
have risen from their beds—
and from blessed slumber part,
impatient for Day to start,
they hear and see for fee.

Jittery Jive

this jumpin' jolt
makes me feel
ALIVE
while I rise

to my edgy edge —
agitation at my best

keyed — UP like a dive
off the high board;

like a frog in the fry pan
I can, I can, I CAN!

Squirrelly
nose-bleed, nose-dive.

The drink depends
on a tiny bean

that satisfies my need
to scurry, sprint, streak.

A little seed
provides the speed —

all from a tiny jumpin' bean.
Know what I mean?

The Coffee Maker

The coffee maker is there
on the counter, its plug
securely in the outlet.

The cup sits dutifully next
to the coffee maker,
awaiting eventual use.

But, where is the coffee?
Where the rich, brown, energizing
gravel filling a pouch or canister?

Here I stand looking
to the coffee maker to create
my morning get-me-up.

But, where is the pick-me-up,
let's-get-going brew that keeps
me running the daily race?

Here, the canister echoes loud.
The air inside, no grounds are found.
I must rely on something new.

Ahhhhh. Tea.

Murder for Tea

I'm planning a tea party
for next Saturday and even now, as I sit
writing the invitations, it feels
obscene. — On TV, I watch the war

in our cities and towns —
one man against another,
neighbors shooting and
looting; throwing rocks through

car windows — and why? For what?
I go out to the garden and
pluck the nasturtiums for
my salad, the pansies for tea

tarts. I smell the garden's
earth turned over;

it's black insides falling
like ropes of intestines
from a mud corpse whose flesh
feeds my crops.

I wish we could stop
the killing. I wonder how I can
be so audacious as to plan
a party when small children

are being murdered in our streets
and the bloodied soil blazes
with vulgarities of one man
against another.

You Can't Always Sit in the Corner Booth

Sometimes you have to belly up
to the counter, clutch your beer and vittles
to your chest while wrestling the bar stool.

Morals fly away. Modesty goes the way of
endangered species — disappearing in the mist
of mayhem and malice.

Integrity is a sentiment. It's a sexually-transmitted
disease with diminishing returns —
Virtue is endlessly indecent, untrustworthy.

Ethical behavior has gone down wind,
like the smoke from a forest fire,
ready to circle back, or dissipate.

Sincerity lurks like the waitress
at your table — waiting for your reply.
Place your order and kiss your future good-bye.

Quenched

I feel self-contained —
no spilling emotion,
no radiating pain,

nothing to light my fiery ire.
There is no other to feign
displeasure until I expire.

No disquiet rolling around
in my head; no news
article providing worry or dread.

I'm copacetic. I'm free.
Contentment
has got the best of me.

One Balmy Evening

Sinking sun low over the western edge
of the stadium glints in and out of rafters.
Food vendors bawl their tune
in time with the pitch—
a swing and a miss.

Waiting for the next pitch,
the noise of the crowd fades,

time stands still as you doze,
then dream some.
The bat crack brings you back.

You sip your brew and smile.
He does too.

The evening, balmy and fair,
you and your spouse—a pair
of fans in matching hats,
similar sentiments that
require not much effort
to share as you stare and
your returning dream

comes true, as you
enjoy the evening
the crowd, the play—

doesn't matter
if your team
loses or wins.

Caravan

Settle near the campfire. Sip
transcontinental Lapsang,
Souchong or Oolong;

aromatic and full-bodied,
it's smokey taste finds you
all the way from the 18th century.

We desert travelers' karwan[6]
resting this winter's night —
notes of pine scent the air.

We anticipate being twenty miles
closer to home by sunset
tomorrow; dream of sleeping

in our own bed, with
the arms of our spouse
draped around.

The stamp and spit of the camels,
amplified five hundred times,
sounds like music in the night.

The journey of this past day reflected
in the evening's dying firelight,
promises offered; promises kept.

[6] karwan — an assembled constituency (India)

Homeward Bound

Homeward bound —
My adventure used up.
Its burnt-out end completing
days in another land.

Homeward bound —
The tale most recently spun.
My family is waiting
to hear the tale unwound.

My last cuppa' waits
with my spouse,
in the house of my desires
where my pleasure lies.

Homeward bound —
journey's end in sight.
Time resumes
its normal flight.

More, Please

This life, like *my* last
cup of coffee,
has been
so full,
so fascinating,
so effervescent,
that when I die,
I shall ask,
"*May I have another?*"

Because you asked . . .

Coffee Cherries

"In fact, the scent of coffee alone has been shown to have energizing effects on the brain"

Joshua Shaffley, "Wake Up and Smell the Coffee"
National Coffee Blog, `nationalcoffeeblog.org`

Pruned short,
grown rich, in soil;
temperate climate — some
sun, but more rain.
Small shrubs to tall trees —
such a variety!

It takes a year
to mature;
then the cherry
offers a full-bodied
aroma and depth
of flavor with
a pronounced sharpness.

Peaberries may be
Sweeter, with more
flavor than standard beans;
the fragrant oil, *caffeol*
locked inside
begins to emerge
during the roasting.
like a summer breeze's
wide expanse.

My Faves

My Coffee Faves

Arabic: has a medium body and sharp acidity, and is often described as having perfect balance.

Robusta: which is strongly aromatic with a light body and acidity.

Brazilian: is clear, sweet, medium bodied, and low acid.

Ethiopian: tends to offer a remarkable and bold statement: full bodied, a bit down to earth.

Kenyan: beans produce a sharp, fruity acidity, combined with full body, and rich fragrance.

Indonesian: known for its fine-aged coffee — has a pronounced rich, full body, and mild acidity.

Vietnamese: coffee with light acidity and mild body has a good balance for blending.

My Tea Faves

Chai: from Turkey, is served in a small glass tulip shaped cup. I love that it uses cinnamon and other spices to create a rich aroma and taste.

Assam: This black tea from England holds its flavor, tastes great early and hot or later with ice and as a late after-supper pick-up.

Oolong (and other green teas): from China, served hot or cold in a small, plain cup or as part of a ceremonial and social occasion. Green teas are lighter in color but hold up with full flavor.

Tea Tisane: is usually a tea made from flowers and/or herbs. This was originally made with barley.

Then, There Is Chocolate!

Chocolate: is a food product made from the fruit of a cacao tree. What kind of magic is that?

Resources

National Coffee Association: https://www.ncausa.org/About-Coffee/Coffee-Health

Ten Thousand Villages: https://www.tenthousandvillages.com

Live Science: https://www.livescience.com/61754-chocolate-facts.html

Publications by Island of Wak-Wak

Sublimation

Volume 1, Issue 1: Trauma ISBN: 979-8326064301 — $11

Volume 1, Issue 2: Awe ISBN: 979-8329443783 — $11

Volume 1, Issue 3: We Are Monsters All ISBN: 979-8333709653 — $11

Volume 1, Issue 4: Every Party Needs a Bard ISBN: 979-8339914266 — $11

Cabin Reading Series

Metamodern Morning Angst and Other Horrors by TS S. Fulk
ISBN: 978-9198959802 — 200 SEK

The Ward at Twilight by Ken Anderson
ISBN: 978-9198959819 — $20

Coffee Table Chapbook Series

Caffeinated by Annette Gagliardi
ISBN: 978-9198959826 — $12

See `www.islandofwakwak.com` for more information and links to where you can order.